The Mentor Kit

by Diane Nash and Don Treffinger

Illustrations by Mark Cavallaro

For Judy and John, of course

ISBN 1-882664-06-X

© 1993, Prufrock Press

Prufrock Press Post Office Box 8813
Waco, Texas 76714-8813
1-800-998-2208

Contents

What an individual can learn and how he learns it depends on what models he has available.

—Seymour Papert

We are beginning to believe what has never ceased to be said: that lessons in lesson-books are not the whole of education.

—Janet Stuart

And gladly wolde he lerne, and gladly teche.

—Chaucer

Preface

Curiously, the mentorship concept receives a standing ovation from ivory towered academe, as well as hard-nosed business realists. And well it should. Very often successful mentorships trigger powerful consequences for both mentor and mentee.

Mentorships, the art of a creatively productive person teaching, counseling, and inspiring a student with similar interests, largely fall into two categories. Some are the result of the accident of circumstance and others are consciously engineered by the academic world (Sarason & Lorentz, 1979). But the chemistry of both types relies on a natural affinity felt by both parties that is characterized by mutual caring, depth, and response (Torrance, 1984).

Perhaps the popularity of academic mentorships can be understood in light of the many winners: mentee, mentor, school, and community. Each seems to enjoy special dividends.

Researchers clearly view the role of mentor as an eclectic one. Boston (1978) sees the advisor, guide, teacher, and competent role model layer. Mattson (1980) adds the notion of tutor, director, advocate, devil's advocate, supervisor, and friend. And Torrance (1984) stresses the builder of self-confidence, developer of thinking skills, and the nurturer of creative growth functions. Indeed, effective mentors are not surrogate teachers required to evaluate, report, and record, but are caring professionals such as scientists, lawyers, photographers, football players, and chefs (Runions, 1980). And very often the student winners in this scenario emerge with significant gains in cognitive areas as well as self-esteem. Not bad.

The mentor gains may appear to be more subtle but they are

often highly meaningful. Mentees often prove to be an added spark in the lives of mentors. Who wouldn't desire an admiring fan with mutual interests? (It is not unusual for a professor serving as a mentor to recount warm and inspiring anecdotes about his or her mentee's progress—as opposed to the stalemate ambiance of his or her own classes.) Mentoring also appeals to man's altruistic streak since everyone knows that teachers and parents can't do the job alone. Ultimately the relationship can produce a network survival mechanism for both parties as the learner matures (Korda, 1984). Torrance's (1984) longitudinal study of 220 young adults (about 30 years old), who grew up in middle class Minnesota families between 1950 and 1980 and attained relatively high levels of education, found 52 percent of the mentorship relationships persisted at the time of follow-up. An impressive record.

Schools benefit in at least three ways. The first is curriculum. The mentorship component adds substantially and creatively to a student's academic experience. The second is recruitment. Schools with established mentorship programs report that these programs are often a "drawing card" for attracting students. The third is in the area of spillover. Often staff members are enriched through their students' participation in mentor programs; very frequently students share information about their adventure with regular classroom teachers. Truly laudable.

These benefits can be summarized as follows:

Benefits of a Mentor

Benefits to the Mentor:
  1. Identifies someone who cares about what you do, as you do.
  2. Allows one to be a bit of a hero.
  3. Develops "survival mechanisms."

Benefits to Schools:
  1. Adds substantively and creatively to student's academic experience.
  2. Serves as "drawing card" for recruitment, public relations.
  3. Encourages spillover—sharing ideas, activities with other teachers and students.

Benefits to Community:
  1. Bridges gap between school and community.
  2. Creates foundation for participation and support.
  3. Promotes civic pride.

Finally, the community benefits too. Mentorships help to bridge the gap between the educational world and its surrounding community. If the bridges are constructed in a sturdy fashion, mutual support follows. And schools that enjoy such support often are a source of tremendous pride. Certainly a desirable goal.

But the gulf between popular praise for the concept and the number of gifted students who actually experience this relationship is dramatic. Hence, the need exists to develop and publish effective mentorship models. We must get beyond the usual pep talk prose often published about isolated mentorship programs and on to examining the nuts and bolts of various programming possibilities.

Enter *The Mentor*. This book reflects our research over 25 different academic models that have successfully connected students of various ages (even the very young!) with mentors. The data collected have been distilled into seven key steps that promote program excellence.

Special emphasis has also been placed on creative problem solving the somewhat predictable headaches that many mentorship programs report. These include program burnout, student drop outs, insufficient numbers of mentors, etc.

Every program knows its own form of migraine. But the excellent programs seem to know how to diagnose the problem and find the cure.

Step One: Agreeing on Definitions

Men-tor (men'tôr', -tər). *Greek Mythology.* Odysseus' trusted counselor under whose disguise Athena became the guardian and teacher of Telemachus. [Latin Mentor, from Greek *Mentor*, name probably meaning "adviser," "wise man." See men-1 in Appendix.*]

men-tor (men'tôr', -tər) *n.* A wise and trusted counselor or teacher: *"Moore and Kierkegaard have become mentors of two different philosophic movements."* [French, from *Mentor* a character in Fénelon's *Telemachus* (1699), modeled after Mentor.]

Figure 1

"The question is," said Alice, "whether you can make words mean so many different things."

—Lewis Carroll

Step One: Agreeing on Definitions

In the Neanderthal stage of program discussions, it will be quite helpful if the participants agree on some basic definitions. Ensuring that everyone is speaking the same language will facilitate communication and save needless (sometimes endless) debate at a later stage.

Often people start out using the same words, but not necessarily "speaking the same language." The terms "mentor," "mentoring," and "mentorship" have appeared in many different ways in articles, books, and brochures describing programs. "Mentorships" have included everything from helpful visits by older students to parents giving slide shows to extended individual internships under the direction of experts. "Mentor program" descriptions range from learning centers about careers to field trips to full-time resident apprenticeships. The words are used in so many different ways that it is really essential for you to begin by clarifying your own beliefs and attaining consensus about working definitions. We hope the Mentor Glossary in this section will be a helpful guide for you.

When we began our work in the project that led to this book, it was with some skepticism. It seemed likely that the current trend toward interest in mentors was just another catchy educational phrase—a fad that "trendy" people and "slick" media would discuss for a year or so.

As we became more involved in reading about programs, studying research and evaluation reports, and talking with people who have been involved in mentorships and mentor programs, the importance of the topic became much clearer.

A strand or theme emerged: the importance of having someone (or a series of someones) who really cares about you, your creative talent, and its development.

This strand, and the powerful role that mentoring can play in it, just could not be dismissed. In his summary of the findings of a 22-year study, Torrance (1984) reported, for example, that persons who have had mentors were more creatively productive than persons who did not have mentors, in relation to both the quantity and quality of their achievements. Those who had mentors also successfully completed more education than those who had not had mentors. The mentor's role has been described in many ways by educational writers and researchers but the common strand is one of the caring nurture of creative talents and accomplishments. Torrance also described many important things the mentor can do for creatively gifted young people. These are summarized in Table 1 on page 10.

The Role of the Mentor

Boston (1978)
Adviser
Guide
Teacher
Competent Role Model

Mattson (1980)
Tutor
Director
Advocate
Devil's Advocate

Torrance (1984)
Builder of Self-Confidence
Developer of Thinking Skills
Nurturer of Creative Growth

Bloom et. al. (1985)
Learning the Language
Learning the History
Learning the Rituals
Learning the Techniques
Professional Skills and Attitudes
Contacts, Opportunities, Choices
Entering the Field/Marketplace

TABLE 1

The Most Important Things Mentors Can Do
For Creatively Gifted Youth

(Torrance, 1984)

Help them to:

1. Be unafraid of "falling in love with something" and pursue it with intensity and in-depth. A person is motivated most to do the things they love and can do best.

2. Know, understand, take pride in, practice, use, exploit, and enjoy their greatest strengths.

3. Learn to free themselves from the expectations of others and to walk away from the games that others try to impose on them.

4. Free themselves to play their own game in such a way as to make the best use of their strengths and follow their dreams.

5. Find some great teachers and attach themselves to these teachers.

6. Avoid wasting a lot of expensive, unproductive energy in trying to be well-rounded.

7. Learn the skills of independence and give freely of the infinity of their greatest strengths.

The Mentor Glossary

In order to promote a common agreement of working terms within an educational community, the following glossary will be a helpful starting point.

APPRENTICESHIP/INTERNSHIP: a short-term, career-oriented experience between a student and a working adult or a group of working adults where the relationship has a distinct business-like slant.

BRAINSTORMING: a "tool" for promoting divergent thinking or producing many ideas. The rules encourage emphasizing quantity rather than quality of ideas; deferring judgment; encouraging unusual ideas; and combining ideas. Having available a long list of alternatives increases the chances of a high-quality solution. (Osborn, 1963; Isaksen & Treffinger, 1985).

BURN OUT: inevitable stress that results from trying to do a complex job alone, without the proper tools and organization; board-of-education support; and building principal and community resource committee back-up. (Even large amounts of the vitamin B complex will not prevent it without these three givens!)

CONTRACT: a written agreement signed by the student and coordinator (perhaps parent and/or mentor) that outlines student goals and responsibilities along with calendar checkpoints. Often a student product and appropriate audience is also identified. One of the best insurance policies available, contracts keep everyone honest and get results.

COMMUNITY RESOURCE COMMITTEE: a committee of teachers, parents, and students (it's hard to say no to kids!) designed to comb through the community for people of all ages who might serve as mentors. This helps build program ownership and heads off coordinator stress.

COORDINATOR: the person whose job title includes responsibility for implementing a mentor model. Special duties may include directing a community resource committee in locating mentors, matching students with mentors, guiding students in the independent study process, coordinating student-mentor schedule, and advertising program successes.

CREATIVE PROBLEM SOLVING: a process that alternates between divergent thinking (imagination) and convergent thinking (judgment) in six steps—mess-finding, data-finding, problem-finding, idea-finding, solution-finding, and acceptance-finding. Educators, students, and parents will find this tool very useful in dealing with a wide variety of challenges. (Isaksen & Treffinger, 1985)

ENRICHMENT VS. ACCELERATION CONTROVERSY: this is a "great debate." Should gifted students be studying the traditional curriculum at a much faster pace (acceleration) or should they be introduced to learning experiences that broaden the existing curriculum (enrichment)? The enriched curriculum places heavy emphasis on critical and creative thinking skills. Mentorships often satisfy both camps as they offer enriched and accelerated learning experiences simultaneously.

FORMS: working documents that expedite the implementation of educational models. Useful forms for mentorship models include student interest checklists, community volunteer recruitment forms, student nomination forms, independent study contracts, product checklists, product evaluation forms, mentorship evaluation forms, and program brochures.

INDEPENDENT STUDY: the process of allowing students to pursue intensely and creatively topics of special interest, using advanced research techniques.

LOG: a diary kept by students during the mentorship that records student activities.

MENTEE: the student in the mentor relationship.

MENTOR: a creatively productive person who teaches, counsels, and inspires a student with similar interests. The relationship is characterized by mutual caring, depth, and response (Torrance, 1984).

MENTOR BANK: a growing list of available people, along with their area of specialty, who might serve as mentors. The specialty areas may be vocational or avocational.

NOMINATION: the process of referring a student who has a burning interest in an area for a mentorship activity. Teachers and program coordinators usually initiate the process. Sometimes parents, peers, and students themselves can also begin the process.

PRODUCTS: student creations that are logical consequences of research done during mentorships. Examples are articles published, computer programs written, films and television produced, brochures designed, professional surveys conducted, etc. Students are motivated by working on products that have a real purpose intended for real audiences! A sample matrix suggesting a variety of products is shown on page 15 (Feldhusen & Treffinger, 1985).

READINESS: the time in a student's development when a mentorship experience is appropriate. When a student shows a sustained interest and creative talent for a given topic; when his or her task commitment and organizational skills have matured sufficiently to handle mentorship requirements; and when a suitable mentor match is available is the time to explore mentor possibilities. This can occur at various points during a student's elementary, secondary, and college career. There is no magic age that is more appropriate than another.

"REAL PROBLEMS" VS. "CONTRIVED PROBLEMS" ISSUE: "canned" student problems are artificially contrived (e.g., write an essay on your summer vacation). Canned problems are the norm in education. Real problems focus on unresolved issues that interest particular students (e.g., design and conduct a professional survey concerning the possible addition of a shopping plaza in your town and present the findings at a town board meeting). Real problems turn kids on! Canned problems may be most valuable when students are initially learning and practicing a problem solving model or method.

TUTOR: a teacher, often financially reimbursed, who teaches general content areas to students for remedial or enrichment purposes.

Are Mentors Only For Gifted And Talented Students?

Our response to this depends once again on your definition of "gifted and talented." If you mean a certain, arbitrary or fixed percentage of students selected primarily by criteria such as IQ or achievement tests, our answer is simply, "No."

On the other hand, if your definition of "giftedness" emphasizes the potentials of students, the strengths and characteristics that can be recognized and nurtured to promote creative productivity, we would be more likely to say, "Yes." In Step Five of this book, we will look more closely at some characteristics of students (and mentors) which might help bring about success. Briefly, students who display specific interests or talent in certain areas, who readily learn new things in those areas, and who exhibit imagination and curiosity, may be good prospects for mentorship experiences. Their thirst for knowledge about their area of interest, intense curiosity, ability to generate ideas, and their high degree of motivation and enthusiasm is likely to be a "spark" to a productive relationship with mentors who bring the same characteristics to their work!

THE A-B-C'S OF STUDENT PRODUCTS

Feldhusen & Treffinger, 1985

A
Advertisement
Advice column
Album
Allegory
Ammonia imprint
Anagram
Anecdote
Animation
Annotated bibliography
Announcement
Anthem
Apparatus
Aquarium
Artifacts
Associations
Audiotapes
Autobiography
Axiom

B
Baked goods
Ballet
Banner
Batik
Beverage
Bibliography
Billboard
Biography
Book
Box
Brochure
Building
Bulletin Board
Business

C
Cartoons
Calendar
Campaign
Case study/Case history
Catalog
Ceramics
Charts
Checklists
Clothing
Club
Code
Collage
Collection
Comedy
Comic Book
Community action/service
Compound
Computer program
Conference
Conference presentation
Convention
Costume
Course of Study
Crossword

D
Dance
Debate
Demonstration
Design
Diagram
Diorama
Directory
Discovery
Display
Drama
Drawing

E
Editorial
Energy saving
    device/plan
Equipment
Estimate
Etching
Eulogies
Experiment

F
Fabrics
Fantasy, science fiction
Fashions
Feature story
Film
Filmstrip
Fiction
Flags
Flannel boards
Food
Formulas
Furniture
Future scenarios

G
Gadgets
Gallery
Game
Garment
Gauge
Gift
Glass cutting
Graph
Graphics
Greeting Cards

H
Handbills
Handbook
Hatchery
Hats
Headlines
"Helper" service
Hieroglyphics
Histories
Hologram
Hot-Line

I
Icons
Ideas
Identification charts
Images
Index
Inscription
Insignia
Instruments
Interviews
Inventions

J
Jamboree
Jazz
Jewelry
Jigsaw puzzle
Jobs
Joke, jokebook
Journal (personal)
Journal article

K
Kaleidoscope
Keepsake
Kit
Knitting

L
Labels
Laboratory
Ladder of ideas
Languages
Latch hooking
Laws
Layouts
Learning centers
Leatherwork
Lei
Lesson
Letter to editor
Library
List
Lithograph
Log
Looking glass
Lounge
Lyrics

M
Machine
Macrame
Magazine
Magic trick
Map
Marquee
Masks
Meetings
Menu
Meter
Mobile
Model
Monument
Mnemonic device
Mural
Museum

N-O
Newsletter
Newspaper
Newspaper ad
News story
Notice
Novel
Oath
Observance
Observatory
Observation record
Occupation
Opera
Opinion
Oration
Orchestration
Organization
Origami
Outline

P
Painting
Pamphlet
Papier maché
Parodies
Patterns
Pennants
Petition
Photograph
Pillow
Plan
Poem
Poster
Prediction
Press release/confe-
    ence
Production
Prototype
Puppet
Puppet show
Puzzle

Q-R
Quarterly report
Query
Question
Questionnaire
Quilling
Quilt
Quiz
Radio program
Rating
Reaction
Recipe
Research report
Resolution
Review
Riddle
Robot
Role playing

S
Satire
Scrapbook
Sculpture
Set/scenery
Short story
Silk screen
Simulations
Skit
Slide show
Slogan
Song
Speech
Stained glass
Steps
Store
String art
Stuffed animal
Survey

T-U
Tape recording
Taxonomy
Television program
Term paper
Terrarium
Test
Theme
Theory
Tie-dyeing
Tool
Tour
Toy
Transparencies
Travelogue
Uniform
Unit of study

V
Vehicle
Verse
Videotape
Vignette
Visual aid
Volume
Volunteer program

W
Walking tour
Wall hanging
Weather map
Weaving
Whittling
Wire Sculpture
Woodcarving
Woodwork
Word games
Written drama

X-Y-Z
Xerographic print, collage
Xylographics
Yardstick
Yarn (story or fabric)
Yearbook
Yodel
Yo-Yo
Zig-Zag
Zodiac
Zones
Zoographic studies
Zoological projects

STEP TWO: APPLYING PERSUASION 101

Speak the speech, I pray you, as I pronounce it to you, trippingly on the tongue.

—Shakespeare

Step Two: Applying Persuasion 101

It can be a formidable challenge to introduce mentorships into the calendar-minded structure of American education. You will need to be a skillful persuader since mentorships deviate curiously from pre-dictable educational protocol. They embrace learning outside textbooks, tolerate teachers who lack certification by state education departments, and sometimes even allow students to solve real world problems (Sarason & Lorentz, 1979). Not exactly the norm! Perhaps this is why a number of well-intentioned programs have merely limped along in a confused state, or even slipped off the mortal coil.

To build a solid foundation for a strong mentor program or to flame interest in a fledgling one, consider using the following three basic arguments with your audience. They work.

1. History—Show the skeptics that mentorships have been important throughout powerful historical examples. You may wish to begin with the etymology of the Greek word mentor. Mentor, as portrayed in Homer's *Oddessy*, was the loyal friend and advisor of Odysseus, king of Ithaca. Entrusted with the education of Odysseus' youngest son Telemachus, Mentor proved to be a wise teacher, counselor, and friend.

Other well known examples throughout history that suggest the profound influence of mentors can be observed in the relationship between Socrates and Plato, Jesus and the Apostles, Aristotle and Alexander the Great, Anne Sullivan and Helen Keller, and Freud and Jung to name a few (Boston, 1976).

Turning to almost any endeavor will reveal high achievers who experienced a mentor at one point in their lives. Korda (1984) writes of Lyndon B. Johnson's career:

It was no accident that Speaker of the House Sam Rayburn took the young Lyndon B. Johnson under his wing when Johnson was still a wet-behind-the-ears assistant to a Texas congressman and mentored him all the way to his own seat in the House, then the Senate, and the Vice-Presidency. "Mr. Sam" saw in Johnson a replica of himself, an awkward, serious-minded country boy with a passion for politics, a hick who could outwit the city slickers from the East without losing the common touch with the folks back home. He made sure that Congressman Johnson got on the best committees, met the important men in the Senate and Congress, brought him to the attention of FDR—and when Johnson became powerful, it's been said he in turn protected Mr. Sam's position as speaker.

Academic research suggests that the most important influence in the lives of high achievers often comes from a mentor. Researchers Goertzel and Goertzel (1962) documented the one-to-one relationship that was the basis for developing outstanding talent in most of their 400 eminent subjects. Conversely three-fifths of their 400 subjects registered dissatisfaction with traditional teachers and classrooms, even though four-fifths showed outstanding talent. (Alas, there were a few exceptions. Martin Luther King Jr., who skipped grades, actually liked school.)

2. Realism—Show that mentorships can bring outstanding resources to a school program at little or no cost. Everyone knows that elementary and secondary libraries pale compared to the substantial Library of Congress and the Chicago and New York City public libraries. High tech enthusiasts immediately understand that taxpayer supported school budgets will never really be able to purchase state-of-the-art equipment. And a close examination of elementary and secondary teacher education programs indicates that teachers have either very general backgrounds or narrow academic specialties. Science teachers rarely conduct pure research; English teachers rarely publish. While existing school resources may be quite high in quality, they are always very limited in scope. Schools must candidly recognize these limitations and understand that there is life outside the classroom. And often it is free for the asking!

3. Success—Show that other places are already implementing mentor programs. Fortunately some fine mentorship models are successfully weathering the education battleground. Offshoots of the Texas A&M Model, the National High School Executive Internship Program, the Mentor Academy and components with the Revolving Door Model (to name a few) are flourishing. The Texas A&M Career Education Model requires a two-hour block of time in a high school student's schedule for a full academic year. It involves a guidance lab for the first quarter of a school year, a mentorship lab with a college university professor for the second quarter and a working internship in onsite work experiences for the third quarter.

The National Executive High School Internship Program is a full-time, one semester pull-out for high school juniors and seniors who work with business professionals at an executive level. It is a national program that provides coordinator training, curricular materials, and technical assistance.

The Mentor Academy Model is a program that builds a mentorship curriculum within the existing high school curriculum. In this program, grade 10-12 students work with a mentor and also become a mentor for elementary students. The Revolving Door Model has spawned numerous situations throughout the country where mentors guide students in the development of "Type IIIs." With this type of activity, students identify an area of advanced level work, focus on a specific problem within this area, use multiple advanced level resources, locate raw data using methodological techniques, develop a polished piece of work, and share products and findings with appropriate audiences.

Since the 1970s, reports of student achievement in mentorship programs are a constant source of delight (National Commission on Youth, 1980). Older students do research for the BBC television productions; they illustrate medical texts; they lobby in state capitals; they co-publish original research done with scientists in professional journals; they write for newspapers; they assist in making executive level decisions. The litany is long and provocative.

Indeed, the future appears to be casting its vote for mentorships. As we move toward an even greater degree of occupational specialization, it is often a mentor who can respond more immediately and satisfyingly to student needs while the dinosaur-like educational institution plods along.

Also, with dramatic shifts in population and work patterns, children are spending increased time with peers and less time with adults. Mentors speak to the needs of kids moving into the 21st century by providing quality time on a one-to-one basis (Nash, 1984).

In short, you can offer your audience arguments rooted in the past, present, and future to underscore your thesis.

STEP THREE:
CULTIVATING CREATIVE
PROBLEM SOLVING

Step Three: Cultivating Creative Problem Solving

People in mentoring relationships are problem solvers!

By the very nature of the process in which we bring people together who have strong interests, talents, and needs, there must be a focus on problem-solving, whether you're a teacher, administrator, program coordinator, parent, mentor, or mentee.

First, if you're considering developing a mentor program in your area or school, you'll have plenty of opportunities to solve problems. There will be the usual challenges—finding planning time, getting busy people to join you, following the steps in this book, etc. (Remember that problem solving can involve working on opportunities and challenges, not just dealing with troubles and concerns.)

But you will probably also encounter your share of both kinds of problems; there will certainly be some unexpected obstacles and undesired roadblocks along the way. And there will certainly be some people who will tell you that it'll never work, ready with their lists of "Idea Killers" (see the "Handy Dandy Checklist" on page 26).

Second, if you are a participant in a mentoring relationship (as a "principal" or even someone giving indirect support or encouragement) there will be a need for problem solving to deal with the day-to-day challenges and dynamics of the relationships; the logistics of schedules, meetings, and deadlines; the stresses of personal relationships and emotional needs; the demands and tensions that arise between our creative interests and the everyday routines of the outside world.

Third, as a mentor or mentee, you will need problem solving skills to apply to the actual content of the work or projects you are doing. Mentors and mentees do not just learn and share presently known, available facts.

They turn their attention and efforts to the unknown: to new questions, puzzling phenomena, unsolved problems that are at the frontiers of their field. Problem solving processes and skills can provide an important and useful set of "tools" and an effective "language" or means of communication. These skills help the mentor and mentee in making progress in their work together, as well as in developing a strong relationship or "bond" with each other.

Many books have been written about problem solving processes and methods. Noller's (1982) *Mentoring: a voiced scarf* gives a step-by-step description of many of the "connections" between mentoring and the creative problem solving (CPS) process.

The CPS model has been used by problem solvers in education, business, and professions for more than 30 years; it is a systematic approach for generating and analyzing new ideas and for developing a "Plan of Action" that will lead to successful implementation of promising new ideas.

The six stages in CPS have been presented in detail in the text, *Creative Problem Solving: the Basic Course* by Isaksen and Treffinger (1985). For our present purposes, we'll summarize those stages very briefly (see Figure 2, page 27) and examine what might be involved in each stage in a mentoring program or relationship.

Handy Dandy Checklist
(How to kill ideas)

1. That idea is silly or ridiculous.
2. We've tried it before.
3. We've never tried it before.
4. It will cost too much.
5. It's not in our area of responsibility.
6. It's too radical a change.
7. We don't have the time.
8. It will make other things obsolete.
9. We're too small to do that.
10. It's not practical in our situation.
11. The community will be upset.
12. Let's get back to reality.
13. That's not our problem.
14. The old way has always worked well.
15. You're two years ahead of your time.
16. We're not ready for it.
17. It isn't in the budget.
18. Can't teach an old dog new tricks.
19. The board (administration, management ...) won't go for it.
20. We'll look foolish if it fails.
21. We've done OK without it.
22. Let's think about it for awhile.
23. Let's form a committee to study it.
24. Has it worked for anyone else?
25. It won't work at our level (or in our area).

Creative Problem Solving Process

Divergent Phase	Problem Sensitivity	Convergent Phase
Experiences, roles and situations are searched for messes ... openness to experience; exploring opportunities.	**Mess Finding** (diverge / converge)	Challenge is accepted and systematic efforts undertaken to respond to it.
Data are gathered; the situation is examined from many different viewpoints; information, impressions, feelings, etc. are collected.	**Data Finding**	Most important data are identified and analyzed.
Many possible statements of problems and subproblems are generated.	**Problem Finding**	A working problem statement is chosen.
Many alternatives and possibilities for responding to the problem statement are developed and listed.	**Idea Finding**	Ideas that seem most promising or interesting are selected.
Many possible criteria are formulated for reviewing and evaluating ideas.	**Solution Finding**	Several important criteria are selected to evaluate ideas. Criteria are used to evaluate, strengthen, and refine ideas.
Possible sources of assistance and resistance are considered; potential implementation steps are identified.	**Acceptance Finding**	Most promising solutions are focused and prepared for action; specific plans are formulated to implement solution.

New Challenges

Source: Isaksen, S.F. & Treffinger, D.J. *Creative Problem Solving: The Basic Course*, 1985, reproduced by permission of Bearly Limited, Buffalo, NY.

Mess-Finding

The first stage involves considering many possible goals or opportunities, and deciding which will be the broad focus for your problem solving efforts.

Examples: After exploring many possibilities, you might select a focus.

Developing a Program	Mentor/Mentee Relations	Working on a Project
Let's create opportunities for students to work with some of our community's really talented people.	How can I be certain that I'll get along with the person I'm going to be working with?	Let's see if we can develop a good way to recognize how young children prefer to learn new things.

Data-Finding

The second stage of CPS involves checking many facts, hunches, impressions, observations, feelings, and questions about the mess, and then deciding which data represent the most important concern for our problem solving efforts.

Examples: After exploring many aspects of the data, you might reach some decisions about the most important focus for your efforts.

Developing a Program	Mentor/Mentee Relations	Working on a Project
We decide that the middle school area is viewed as the most promising focus for our program.	Most of our data suggest that we need to select and match mentors and mentees very carefully.	We discover we are most interested in studying young children through observing their behavior.

Problem-Finding

In this stage, the most important direction(s) from data-finding are selected and the search begins for more specific problem statements. The goal is to select a problem statement that expresses the central issue or "the essence" of the situation and will facilitate generating new ideas. (Problem statements usually begin with the phrase, "In what ways might ..." (IWWM) to emphasize the need to generate many ideas.)

Examples: After exploring many possible problem statements, you might select.

Developing a Program	Mentor/Mentee Relations	Working on a Project
IWWM we develop opportunities for mentor relationships?	IWWM I locate promising partners for these relationships?	IWWM we observe pre-schoolers learning preferences?

Idea-Finding

Once a question (or "problem statement") that expresses the essence of our interests and concerns has been selected, the next step is to generate many possible ways that question might be answered. Deliberate efforts are made to produce many new and unusual ideas. Then one or more "promising possibilities" will be chosen for further evaluation and refinement.

Examples: After considering many responses for the question you selected in problem-finding, you might decide that these seem most promising.

Developing a Program	Mentor/Mentee Relations	Working on a Project
Have a talent festival to make students aware of opportunities; Develop a mentor pool.	Arrange for mutual interviews; Set up "trial periods" so placements can be changed.	Station several observers unnoticed at playgrounds; Work with area daycare centers and schools.

Solution-Finding

Promising ideas must be analyzed carefully to screen them (or recognize possible weak points), support them (or refine and develop ideas), or select them (prioritizing and choosing). Solution-finding guides the selection of ideas that have the greatest potential for successful use or action. Specific criteria are used to analyze the ideas and determine advantages, limitations, and unique features about each idea.

Examples: For the idea-finding choices, you might next use specific criteria to study each promising possibility, noting each idea's advantages, limitations, and unique features. Below are samples of how this might be done for one of the ideas from each example.

Developing a Program

The talent festival has the advantage of being able to expose many students to possible mentors. One limitation may be that the contact may be superficial. The program is unique because it might generate interest among both the students and the mentors in the school and community.

Mentor/Mentee Relations

"Trial periods" have the advantage of giving both parties the freedom to change. It is unique because most times students and teachers are "stuck" with each other. A limitation might be that some students or mentors might become frustrated if they have trouble finding partners.

Working on a Project

Observers on the playgrounds has the advantage of not being too obvious. It is unique because it observes children in natural, spontaneous settings. One limitation might be that parents would become suspicious of strangers hanging around the playground regularly.

Acceptance-Finding

There's a difference between "good" ideas and "successful" ideas! In acceptance-finding, the most promising possible solutions for the problem become the basis for planning successful action. A specific plan of action is developed, with steps that will help ensure that the ideas will work.

Examples: After considering the advantages, limitations, and unique features of one or more promising ideas, you might work on "building up" the strengths and overcoming the limitations. After considering possible sources of assistance or resistance, you will decide on a plan of action. For our examples, you might include these steps.

Developing a Program	Mentor/Mentee Relations	Working on a Project
Invite possible mentors to come for a day, make presentations, and visit classes for discussion. Ask each presenter to provide biographical sketches and advance material for students. Arrange for small group follow-up sessions with sign-up sheets.	Explain trial period concept to all mentors/mentees in advance, using "contacts." Have an initial meeting with all trial groups to deal with communication and "team-building" skills. Plan ways to offer data and conferences before placements.	Hold information meetings in communities before observing. Give observers identification badges or unique clothing. Use observers who are known to area parents. Schedule observations in nice weather. Offer training program for observers.

STEP FOUR:
DESIGNING THE ELUSIVE
PERFECT MODEL

The best way to have a good idea is to have lots of ideas.

—Linus Pauling

Step Four: Designing the Elusive Perfect Model

When the time arrives to build a unique mentor model that works for your system, it is also time to promote grassroots ownership. Brainstorming the 50 issues included in the *Mentor Planner* will help to develop a high quality program that is sensitive to student needs, enjoys longevity, and earns public acclaim.

Acceptance-finding, the final CPS step, should be applied at this stage. Planners need to ask the hard questions:

* What obstacles or objections will be raised? By whom?

* Who will help us?

* Who will hinder us?

* Who will gain the most from the program?

* Who will gain the least from the program?

Acceptance-finding involves brainstorming many alternatives that address anticipated problems and then weaving the best of them into a creative plan-of-action.

Expect objections about the following issues to surface in early program development:

* budget concerns

* insufficient student time

* perceived lack of mentors

* liability issues

- lack of teacher awareness

- transportation problems

- threatened teacher unions

- pull-out issues

- student dropouts

- loose criteria for screening and match making

- unsatisfactory mentorship experience based on overly high or low expectations of student performance

- confidentiality on job site issues

- inability of mentor programs to prove cognitive student growth

- public mental set that does not recognize youth's ability

Your anticipating the loyal opposition will make your responses to *The Mentor Planner* even richer.

After confronting some of the bitter issues acceptance-finding introduces, you will be ready to use the *Mentor Matrix*. This matrix reflects an analysis of existing program variables based on a study of 25 programs that fall somewhere within the K-12 framework. These programs were initiated both in public and private schools.

Since this is a morphological matrix, by creatively rearranging the columns there exist more than 160,000 possible ways to design a mentorship program. Somewhere in this matrix exists the secret for your elusive perfect model.

The Mentor Planner

Students:

1. What type of advertising might be used to attract students to the program?

2. Who are the various people who might nominate students for this program?

3. What form of screening will be used to select qualified students?

4. What age/grade levels of students might we service?

5. What methods might we employ to ensure a good "match" between mentor and mentee?

6. What components might be built into the program to address individual student needs and to ensure a high quality experience for the student?

Coordinator:

1. From what background will the coordinator be selected? i.e., classroom teacher, counselor, G/T specialist, administrator, BOCES type coordinator, independent coordinator, volunteer coordinator?

2. What training will the coordinator receive?

3. What budget will the coordinator have?

4. What support base will the coordinator have?

5. What will be the coordinator-student ratio?

6. How often will the coordinator meet with students?

7. How will the coordinator monitor student progress?

8. What skills will the coordinator foster within students? i.e., original research, creative problem-solving, leadership, etc.

9. How will the coordinator continually advertise and promote the program?

Mentor:

1. How will the word mentor be defined?

2. What special training or preparation will the mentor be given?

3. How will the mentor be utilized effectively? i.e., one-to-one with students, advisor to teachers and student, consultant for curriculum, real problem-solving, real audiences, etc.

4. What types of mentors will best serve the program? i.e. university professors, working professionals, craftsmen, housewives, senior citizens, students, etc.

5. Will community talent miners and similar instruments be used to find mentors?

6. What strategies will be used to discover and recruit potential mentors?

7. Will a mentor bank be established? If so, how will it be replenished?

8. What community resources exist that might provide mentors?

9. Will mentors be paid?

10. How will mentors be recognized for their efforts?

Program:

1. Will the program have a special focus? i.e., leadership, arts, social sciences, careers, etc.

2. What special skills will be fostered?

3. In what ways will this educational opportunity be qualitatively differentiated for students?

4. What will be the length of the mentorship?

5. Will students be encouraged to shop around for a mentor?

6. When during a student's schedule will it take place? i.e., entire semester pull-out, one day a week pull-out, one period per day, half day, weekends, evenings, summers, spontaneously, etc.

7. Where will the site of the mentorship be?

8. Will there be a required contract?

9. Will a student log be mandated?

10. Will a student product be required?

11. Will students receive academic credit?

12. How will students leaving the building be transported?

13. How will insurance issues be resolved?

14. Will there be a special sequence involved in the curriculum?

15. Will there be scheduled meetings between mentor and coordinator?

16. Will there be a guidance seminar for all students?

17. Will the mentor program be fused into a larger gifted program or will it have a separate identity?

18. Will the gifted program be a part of the regular school program?

19. Will the program become a distinct "selling card" for the school?

20. Will the program be based on an existing mentorship model or educational model?

21. Will students have an opportunity for a second mentorship experience?

22. Will the program encourage greater flexibility than already exists in student scheduling?

23. How will the program be evaluated?

While mentor models have been designed in many ways, successful ones include a healthy number of the following:

1. Appropriate screening and matching procedures.

2. Identified coordinator with flexible schedule.

3. Rich menu of mentor opportunities.

4. Strong support base, including: Committee, Principal, and Board of Education.

5. Regular counseling time built in to monitor student progress.

6. Various research and process skill instruction blended into program.

7. Evaluation by mentor, student, coordinator, and parent.

8. Allowance for spontaneous development of mentorships throughout the year.

9. Effective public relations campaign.

10. Much hard work and some luck, too!

The Mentor Matrix

WHO?	WHEN?	MENTOR?	LOCATIONS?
Specific grade levels	School day pull-out	College professor	Elementary school
All elementary students	Before school	K-12 teachers	Middle school/Jr. High
Middle/Jr. High students	After school	Craftsmen	High school
Junior college students	At breakfast	Tradespeople	University
Undergraduates	Evenings	Business executives	Junior college
Graduate students	One day a week	High school students	Library
Underachieving students	Weekends	College students	Mentor's home
Gifted-general academic	Full semester pull-out	Senior citizens	Student's home
Visual/Performing Arts	One week pull-out	Housewives/husbands	Business setting
Scientifically talented	Summer	Civic leaders	Cultural setting
Vocationally talented	Early release schedule	Research scientists	Civic setting
Leadership talented	Block scheduling	Medical professional	Media setting
Inner-city students	Winter recess	Legal professional	Cooperative ed. agency
Rural students	Spring recess	Engineering professional	Telephone exchanges
Suburban students	Lunch hour	Media professional	Research institute
Psycho-motor talented	Recess or free period	Artist	Studio
History/Social Science	Study hall	Writer	Summer institute/camp
Reading/Language Arts	Random Sessions	Musician	Coordinator's home
Mathematically talented	Intermittent sessions	Architect	Hospitals
High School students	One month pull-out	Athlete	Courtrooms

The Mentor Matrix

WHO?	WHEN?	MENTOR?	LOCATIONS?

STEP FIVE: SEARCHING SYSTEMATICALLY FOR MENTORS

I get by with a little help from my friends.

—The Beatles

Step Five: Searching Systematically for Mentors

It's true. Many a floundering mentorship program suffers from perceiving a shortage of mentors, working in isolation, and burning out coordinators too easily.

Recruiting of mentors is most profitable when it is approached systematically. Your mentor bank can grow year by year until it is indeed rich. But clearly teamwork is the key.

One prototype that results in effective recruitment is a community resource committee. On the elementary level, membership might include the G/T specialist, a primary teacher, an intermediate teacher, a special area teacher, two parents, a student, and the principal. On the secondary level, membership might include the G/T specialist, core area and special area teachers, parents, students, principal, and counselor. This brainstorming "think tank" group could invite people from the following sources to serve as mentors (or guest speakers):

1. Area college and university professors

2. K-12 teachers

3. Service groups and community organizations such as the Rotary, Lions Club, League of Women Voters, etc.

4. Research institutes

5. Cultural institutes: art, science, music, history, etc.

6. Government agencies

7. Media: television, radio, newspaper, publishing, advertising

8. Area businesses

9. Area libraries

10. Sports organizations

11. Outdoor/environmental associations

12. Professions: medicine, law, education, engineering, literature, architecture, art, etc.

13. Senior citizens

14. K-12 and college students

15. Instructors of credit-free courses

The mass mailings of recruitment letters to community members, as well as ads in local newspapers asking for mentor volunteers, are likely to generate some responses—the number who respond seems to be directly proportional to the age and visibility of the program. *The Community Talent Miner*, designed by Reva Jenkins and Emily Stewart, is a tool commonly used for this purpose.

A direct and highly fruitful approach is to ask committee members, parents, and administrators to make speeches on behalf of building a mentor bank. These people can appear before community service groups, PTAs, high school student councils, National Honor Societies, etc., and ask for community resource volunteers. They can simultaneously teach the gifted education model to the community which can bring future support to the program at critical points in program development.

(One highly organized coordinator reports regularly using the assistance of Toastmaster, an international speakers organization, to help build his mentor bank.) If speeches include slides of students already connecting with community members in a variety of circumstances, audience support will be even greater. Using the *Community Connector* form at this point will prove highly profitable. In using this form, it is important to collect them at the same meeting since people often forget to mail them in.

Once volunteers begin to appear, a computerized list of their specialties can be distributed to staff members in order to promote the utilization of the mentor bank. The list should be updated—perhaps by students with an advanced interest in computers. Software such as Apple Works with its database and word processing for the Apple computer and Personal Record Keeping for the Texas Instruments computer are available.

It is important for volunteers to understand that the inclusion of their name and expertise in a mentor bank does not guarantee that they will be called upon in any given year to help. They should know that the utilization of community resources will be based on student need and teacher request.

In short, an organized speakers bureau, dedicated to building a rich community mentor bank, can be a powerful machine. And it sure beats doing it alone.

The Community Connector

Those having torches will pass them on to others.
                                        —*Plato,* Republic

Name(s) __Jerry Jameson__

Occupation __University Professor — Computer Science__

Address __683 Hilltop Lane, East Aurora 10683__

Home Phone __555-1234__   Business Phone __555-5678__

Areas of Interest: Indicate where possible whether lecture, demonstration, display, discussion, slides/movies, simulation, or "hands-on" activity is possible.
    __Computer Programming__
    __Demonstration Possibilities__
    _____

Amount of time you would be willing to devote:
(single session, several sessions, preferred length)
Number of students you prefer: 1 ____ 2-4 ____ 5-10 _✔_ 10+ ____
Grade or age preferred __Junior High or High School__

When would you be available to work with students?
After school ___ ; Evenings ____ ; During day _✔_; Saturdays ____
Best day(s) of week: __Fridays__
Best time to call: Home __Evening after 6__ Work __Anytime — Days__

Other information:
If you are a local resident, what is the name of the school nearest you?

Elementary School _____
Middle School _____
High School __Franklin Sr. High__

If you are currently a high school student, what high school do you attend and in what year will you graduate? _____

What do we look for in Mentors and Mentees?

At first, you may be fearful that if you're too fussy in your search for mentors, you won't find any. You may be concerned that if it sounds as if you're too demanding, you'll scare away many promising but busy mentors.

We believe, however, that it's important to keep in mind that mentors are people, too, and that they will be involved in relationships with your students that will be sustained and demanding. Good intentions, and the novelty and appeal of helping a young person, may not be sufficient to ensure a successful relationship. It seems likely that, if we raise some important questions at the beginning, we may be able to improve our chances for success.

Similarly, just as there may be some characteristics of mentors who will be successful with students, we should also look closely at the characteristics and skills that will be important for the mentees. Some of the characteristics that we suspect (but cannot prove) may help promote success are listed in the table below.

Torrance (1984) also described, from his 22-year longitudinal research study, a number of factors that have caused mentor relationships to break down or die. These included:

- Intimidation in the relationship ("overpowering" or abusing power)

- Pace too fast or too slow

- Observing sacrifices to personal integrity

- Mentors too limited in outlook or perspective

- Personal barriers (sex, roles, race)

- Mentee's behavior not approved by mentor

- Philosophy of life incompatible with having a mentor

- Separation of mentorship area and earning a living

- Aversion to educational institutions

- Mentee's originality threatens mentor

- Feelings of mistreatment and hurt

- Geographical distances

- Unsuccessful experience with a mentor

- Creating an unconventional career

What to look for in a mentor who will work with children/teens	**What to look for among students who are considering seeking a mentor**
- Comfortable with young people - Some personal experience with young people - Able/willing to commit time - In-depth knowledge of area - Poses new questions/research - Concern for safety - Suggests ideas for school or student contributions - Experts may nominate others who can extend/expand opportunities - Sensitive in formulating expectations for students - Communication skills - Willing to recognize, overcome potential problems - Perceives potential benefits - Many new ideas to investigate, sees future possibilities and consequences - Constructive sense of evaluation	- Sustained curiosity and interest - Ability to focus and exert extended effort on tasks of personal interest - Many questions not being answered by classes or present curriculum - Not challenged by traditional methods and activities - Evidence of active involvement (products, accomplishments, active participation in area) - Current indicators of interest (reading, writing themes) - Extensive vocabulary in field - Satisfactory communication skills with adults - Receptive to new ways of learning - Knows/will learn process and methodological skills - Displays personal sense of responsibility and autonomy

Is training necessary? Possible?

Many people are afraid to suggest that any training might be necessary for either mentors or students before or during a mentorship experience. These fears stem from the same concerns we mentioned in the preceding section: fear of "turning off" the mentor or the student, or fear of "imposing" on leaders who are already maintaining very busy schedules. In addition, some fear that any attempt to provide training will lead to making the relationship too formal, impersonal, or pedantic—"too much like school."

We believe, however, that it may actually be more of an imposition and threat, for both the mentor and the student, if we expect them to be solely responsible for the success or failure of the experience, without offering them some simple support and useful learning experiences that would improve their chances of success. This does not mean that we have to impose "classes" or formal training programs on potential mentors or mentees.

Rather, we believe that effective coordination of a mentor program should involve consultation, assistance, and support in a number of important areas that may be new for the mentor as well as for the mentees. These include:

- Goal Setting and Problem Development

- Problem Solving Methods and Techniques

- Shared Leadership Skills

- Active Listening Methods

- Honest Sharing and Communication Skills

- Understanding of Personal Style and Preferences

- Ability to Share Strengths, Provide and Receive Feedback

- Responding Constructively to Limitations

- Realistic Evaluation of Outcomes and Results

The coordinator's role does not end with the mentor/mentee match. We found that continued communication among coordinators, mentors and mentees produced the highest quality experiences. Students needed to be able to share their new experiences with the coordinator; mentors needed both guidance and encouragement. Formal meetings with the mentors may or may not be possible, but you should maintain good lines of communication through personal visits or telephone calls.

STEP SIX:
APPLYING
THE NECESSARY
WEED AND FEED
FOR PROGRAM GROWTH

The hardest part of raising children is teaching them to ride bicycles ... A shaky child on a bicycle for the first time needs both support and freedom. The realization that this is what the child will always need can hit hard.

—Sloan Wilson

Perhaps ... (independent study) would be a good type of training for any student, bright or dull, but for the gifted student at least, it is the only way that truly educates.

—Louis Terman

Step Six: Applying the Necessary
Weed and Feed for Program Growth

Matching mentors with mentees is both science and art. Alas, a common interest in the same field will not always provide the necessary glue for a productive mentor-mentee bond. Memorize this point. Frequently a coordinator feels personal frustration and guilt if a mentorship seems to fizzle, when it's inevitable that a few will. As John Kennedy once said, "When you have 7 percent unemployed, you have 93 percent working."

Nevertheless, there are established procedures that produce excellent results most of the time. They include:

1. Encouraging students who display high levels of enthusiasm for a guest speaker or mini-course instructor to explore the possibility of a mentor relationship. One coordinator working for a cooperating educational agency reported that her mini-course instructors taught a condensed version of the mini-course to teachers who nominated students for participation in the mini-course component. This promoted teacher ownership for the project. And a particularly excited student taking the mini-course would then be encouraged to consider a mentorship with the instructor. Usually the chemistry was right. At any rate, staff members should be inserviced so that they are clearly looking for turned on students.

2. Allowing students (particularly older ones) to shop around and visit a number of potential mentors. This can be accomplished subtly. Students might conduct career information interviews or write articles for the school newspaper as they simultaneously test their enthusiasm for potential mentors. Even a motivated, organized third grader with help can field this beautifully.

3. Involving students' parents in decision making concerning appropriate mentors. One fairly structured secondary program encourages parents to help their children shop around for a mentor so that potential mentors are already lined up as the fall semester begins. This not only eases the mentor match process for the coordinator but greatly enhances parent support for the program.

4. Including the teachers of students in decision making concerning appropriate mentors. Historically teachers who nominate students are simply more supportive of the program, and if pull-out is an issue, cooperate more fully in compacting curriculum.

5. Promoting the use of public awareness brochures, student contracts and student logs. Of all the forms associated with mentorships, the contract is the most universally used and important. Be sure to use one. It gives structure to freedom and ushers in the highest quality results by keeping everyone honest.

6. Monitoring student progress at established checkpoints. This can be done individually via the telephone or in weekly structured seminars attended by a number of mentees. Mentees need to discuss their mentorship highs and lows; they also need help with interpersonal skills as well as the further structuring of this open-ended experience.

As soon as the relationship is launched, the use of a contract like the *Mentor Contract* or the *Project Checklist* should begin; excerpts from both forms are provided.

The Mentor Contract

Focus of research and responsibilities:

Collection, recording, analysis of data regarding new product growth

Skills:

chart making
computer use

Resources (including scholarly and professional) to be utilized:

— Mr. Jerry Jameson, college computer professor
— Mrs. Margaret Worth, school librarian
— Mr. John Roberts, president of Chamber of Commerce
— Mr. Thomas Holmes, president of Arco Industries
— computer

Appropriate product and audience:

chart for display at local bank

Plan of Action

Mentee Jim Smith will assist with the research and development of a new Arco product. With the help of Professor Jameson, he will collect, record, analyze data regarding a product's growth compared with that of industries in other communities. Determined through computer analysis, the results will be plotted on a chart and displayed in local banks.

Approximate beginning date __9/10__   **Ending date** _12/15_

Meeting dates with coordinators:

Dates & Times	Comments
9/10 - 8:30a.m.	Project goals established
9/17 - 11 a.m.	Planning session with Prof. Jameson
9/26 - 1:30 p.m.	Data collection at Arco Industries
10/3 - 8:30 a.m.	Analysis of data with Prof. Jameson

Evaluation on a scale of 1-10 (1=Poor, 10=Excellent)

Criteria for evaluation	Student evaluation	Teacher evaluation
worked well independently	9	10
used a wide variety of resources	8	8
located scholarly resources	9	9
managed time and resources well	9	8
arranged for completion and sharing of product	10	10
provided bibliographic documentation	10	10
other chart	10	10

There are also pages in the mentor contract for written evaluations by the mentor, mentee, and coordinator.

Project Checklist

Name of Project Director   James Smith

Date Started   9/10

1. **Introduction.** You have been appointed project director for a project of your own. As you work on the project, you're becoming a specialist. You will have special knowledge and experience about your topic. In fact, when you're finished with the project, you will have done more interesting things, and you'll know more about it, than anyone else in your class—and quite possibly more than anyone else in the whole school!

   This project checklist is a guide, to help you plan your project and carry it out successfully.

2. **What's your project?**

   Fill in the title of your project:
       New Product Growth Chart

   Give a brief description of what your project will be about:
       I will collect, record and analyze data regarding a new product's growth. This will be compared with that of industries in other communities. Determined through computer analysis, the results will be plotted on a chart and displayed in local banks.

   What are some of the specific questions your project will investigate?
   — new growth frequency of identified product
   —new growth frequency of identified product in other communities
   —computer analysis of collected data

3. Project Consultants

Remember, you do not have to do this entire project all by yourself! There may be other people who will be able to assist you with the various parts of your project. We call these people consultants.

Here's a list of some people who might help you. In front of each name, there are two boxes. One is for you to check now, to make a note of some people you think might help you. Write their names in the spaces provided, if you wish. The second box is for you to check later, so you will be able to have a record of who really did give you help during the project.

There are also some blank lines for you to fill in the names of other people who may help you during the project.

You may come back to this step later—as often as necessary— to add names or bring it up to date.

❑ ❑ Teacher: _Mrs. Greenheld_   ❑ ❑ Teacher:_____
☑ ❑ Parent: _Andrew_   ❑ ❑ Parent:_____
❑ ❑ Friend: _Michael_   ❑ ❑ Friend:_____
❑ ❑ Librarian: _Mrs. Worth_   ❑ ❑ Librarian:_____
☑ ❑ Business: _Mr. Roberts_   ❑ ❑ Business: _Mrs. Holmes_
❑ ❑ _Professor Jameson_   ❑ ❑ _____
❑ ❑ _____   ❑ ❑ _____

4. Meeting Dates

Use these spaces to keep a record of the meetings you have with the consultants who are assisting you. It would be a good idea to write down the date, the name of the person or people with whom you met, and a brief summary of what decisions you made in your meeting. (Add extra pages if you need them.)

Date	Met With	Decisions We Made
9/10	Mr. Jameson	Use computer to collect data
9/17	Mr. Shafter	Agreed to use display
9/26	Mr. Roberts	Collect data at Arco Industries

5. **Locating and Using Information.** Here are some ideas about how to locate and use some information for your project. In each list, there are two boxes. Your consultants may suggest that you use some of these ideas, by making checks in the first box. You can keep track of the ones you're using by placing checks in the second set of boxes. (Of course, you may check and use some things that your consultants didn't check—that's up to you.)

5a. Things to read/hear/view

❏ ❏ encyclopedia
❏ ❏ dictionaries
❏ ❏ textbooks
❏ ❏ biographies
❏ ❏ magazines
☑ ❏ almanacs
❏ ❏ bibliographies
☑ ❏ library card catalog
❏ ❏ other books

❏ ❏ picture file
☑ ❏ charts
☑ ❏ graphs
❏ ❏ study packets
☑ ❏ records
❏ ❏ radio/TV programs
❏ ❏ newspapers
❏ ❏ maps
☑ ❏ _computers_

5b. Places to go

❏ ❏ library
❏ ❏ historical places
☑ ❏ business places
❏ ❏ concert
❏ ❏ antique shop
❏ ❏ high school
❏ ❏ art gallery
❏ ❏ public buildings
❏ ❏ shopping center
❏ ❏ _____

❏ ❏ town hall
❏ ❏ museums
❏ ❏ outdoors
❏ ❏ theater
☑ ❏ research laboratory
☑ ❏ college or university
❏ ❏ zoo
❏ ❏ office building
❏ ❏ park
☑ ❏ _bank_

5c. People to see/call/write

❏ ❏ teachers
❏ ❏ state officials
☑ ❏ business
❏ ❏ musician
☑ ❏ professor
☑ ❏ librarian
❏ ❏ lawyer
❏ ❏ _____

❏ ❏ town officials
❏ ❏ national officials
❏ ❏ travel agent
❏ ❏ artist
❏ ❏ scientist
❏ ❏ reporter
❏ ❏ accountant
☑ ❏ _bank manager_

6. **Possible Products.** Here are some ideas for various products that might be the result of your project. These are different ways you might consider for sharing your project with other people. In the first box, you (with your consultants) can check some of the possibilities. Then, later, you can check the ones you've actually selected in the second set of boxes. (Some projects may have one product; others might lead to several products.)

☑❏ picture essay   ❏ ❏ magazine article
❏ ❏ model to display   ❏ ❏ diorama
❏ ❏ mural/painting   ❏ ❏ record
❏ ❏ tape recording   ❏ ❏ videotape program
❏ ❏ film   ❏ ❏ filmstrip
❏ ❏ slide/tape set   ❏ ❏ oral report
☑❏ posters   ❏ ❏ bulletin board
❏ ❏ newspaper story   ❏ ❏ play
❏ ❏ book or story   ❏ ❏ written research report
❏ ❏ sculpture   ❏ ❏ song/music
❏ ❏ school display   ❏ ❏ presentation at a
❏ ❏ campaign in our town/state/county   meeting of ——————
☑❏ _chart_____   ❏ ❏ _____
❏ ❏ ——————————————   ❏ ❏ _____

7. **Planning Your Product(s).** In these spaces, write down some specific plans about your product and how you might be able to share it with others.

_____ _chart analysis results with artist_ _____
_____
_____
_____
_____
_____

8. Collecting and Organizing Your Data.

After you have read what you need to read, visited the places of importance for your project, talked with the people whom you selected, and selected the kind of product(s) you will use for sharing your work, you need to be sure your material is well-organized.

Here are some resources you might use to help you organize your information and material: check those you're using.

_____ topic outline

✔ a list of main ideas

_____ questions and answers about your subject

_____ tape recorded notes and interviews

_____ file cards to record important ideas

✔ a list of the important steps in preparing your product

_____ picture or slide file in sequence

✔ rough draft of your product

9. Getting Ready for Sharing Your Product.

There are several questions you should be able to answer "yes" before your product is finished. Look over this list as a review before you complete your work. (Not every question will apply for every kind of product.) Check off the questions when you can answer "yes."

✔ Have I used many resources?
✔ Am I sure my information is accurate?
✔ Is the information concise and to the point?
✔ Have I eliminated unnecessary material?
___ Do I feel comfortable with the subject?
___ Have I organized my material in a logical sequence?
___ Have I considered some especially interesting information to get the audience's attention?
___ Am I using interesting charts, graphs, or illustrations?
___ Can I "try out" my product with someone before it's finished?
___ If I'm presenting, have I rehearsed my talk?
___ Do I state my conclusions clearly and specifically?
___ Have I arranged for all the materials I'll need?
___ Do I know my deadlines?
___ Is my project acceptable in size or length for the audience?
___ Have I kept an extra copy for my own records?

10. Sharing Your Project. Use this space to keep a record of how, when, and where you have shared the results of your project.

When?	How?	Where?
12/15-3/4	Charts on easels	in banks

11. Evaluating Your Products.

After you have shared your project with others, you should ask, "How do I feel about the product?" Try to make a list of these things.

——What things did you like best about this project and your products? (Try to find several things.)

✔ What things did you like least about your project and products? (List several.)

✔ Make a list of several things you will change or do in a different way the next time you share this project (or a future project) with an audience.

✔ Make a list of helpful suggestions you have received from your consultants, or from the audiences for your products which will help you improve the products.

12. Where Do We Go From Here?

The most interesting thing about some projects is that answering one group of questions leads to a whole new set of questions and ideas. To conclude your checklist for this project, make a list of some new questions for future projects on this subject. Check some you especially hope to work on.

write a report

offer suggestions for other product analysis

Date of completion of this project: _____

The Mentor Contract does not include a report card section on the mentor. It could have. Certainly some fulfill their roles better than others. But unless the mentor is being reimbursed (only 2 of the 25 programs in our study paid their mentors) the structure did not seem to encourage mentor training sessions. Hence, we are largely dealing with creatively productive people who already lead a hectic, roller coaster existence. Nevertheless, coordinators and researchers have given thought to specific mentor functions. One independent community agency that sponsors mentorships uses this entry in a mentor evaluation form that it asks students to fill out.

Put an X in the areas your mentor was most helpful. Put an O in the areas where the mentor needs the most improvement.

Available (willing to help me when I needed help)

Understanding and patient

Good sense of humor

Enthusiastic about his/her work

Able to teach me many new things

Keeps his/her appointments with me (on time)

Keeps other commitments to me

Allows independence (willingness to let me make decisions about my work)

Tolerance (willingness to let me make mistakes as I learned)

Gives clear instructions and directions

Is able to relate to young people

The Mentor Checklist provides formal guidelines for those mentors seeking further suggestions.

The Mentor Checklist

The mentor's task with respect to the independent learner might include:

1. Exposure to many possibilities.

2. Promoting question-asking.

3. Willingness to listen.

4. Being alert to mentee's interest.

5. Finding resources and cutting red tape.

6. Pointing direction and raising probing questions.

7. Sharing resources from personal files, experiences.

8. Introducing mentee contacts.

9. Establishing opportunities for team effort.

10. Providing constructive criticism from varied perspectives.

11. Helping mentee develop standards.

12. Assisting in revising and polishing.

13. Awareness of internal and external funding opportunities.

14. Helping mentee prepare presentations of work.

15. Finding appropriate audiences for work.

16. Giving feedback in a dress rehearsal process.

17. Serving as a model of productive behavior.

18. Allowing for "tag along" opportunities at conferences, conventions and other professional situations.

19. Creating opportunities for sharing feelings and reactions.

20. Acknowledging obstacles and facing them candidly.

21. Capitalizing on concerns by seeking ways to make them productive.

22. Helping learner recognize and accept the possibility of changes in plans or goals and thereby maintaining flexibility.

23. Maintaining a sense of humor during periods of creative production.

24. Keeping time commitments and other commitments.

25. Encouraging the learner in new directions once the established goals have been achieved.

Outlining mentor functions, Margaret Cellerino (1983) writes:

When working with a student the mentor will act as a guide, share knowledge, demonstrate method of inquiry, give direction, and provide continued support.

The Mentor Contract also assumes that the involved parties have nailed the mentee's greatest interests. If this is an issue with a particularly fuzzy student, consider using Dr. Joseph Renzulli's open-ended interest-a-lyzer or Janice Eichberg and Lindy Redmond's extensive checklist of 1,200 interest areas found in *Choosing and Charting* (1984).

Finally, you may wish to keep records of completed mentor contracts through the years in order to trumpet them at future awareness sessions. Certainly nothing succeeds like success.

Copies of successful mentor contracts should also be included in a student's school file. Future educators and college admissions officers will better understand a student's demonstrated ability with this documented achievement.

If you need a formal evaluation form, a sample has been provided for you.

STEP SEVEN: ADVERTISING THE PRODUCT

The medium is the message.

—Marshall McLuhan

Step Seven: Advertising the Product

It is not only smart to advertise, it may be a necessity. The advertising component in your program should do two things: tell the public that a program exists and tell the public that the program is successful.

You can make it a line item in your budget—one of the 25 programs regularly advertises in *The New York Times* to recruit students for its summer session—or you can turn to the humble purple ditto master and still get fine results. But using any logical combination of the following approaches to recruit for your program or to reflect program successes will be an important finishing touch.

1. Slide shows of current mentorships.

2. Audio and videotaped enthusiastic student testimonials of their positive experiences.

3. Feature articles in local and school newspapers.

4. Newsletters and annual reports.

5. Year end "hoopla" award winners and/or teas honoring mentors and recognizing student achievement.

6. A brochure that highlights program components.

In the event that this list seems awesome at first, you may wish to find a public relations mentor of your own. Somewhere in your backyard lurks a David Ogilvy willing to help your worthy cause. At any rate, try not to do the job alone.

Distributing a mentor brochure serves to educate everyone

involved in the process as well as the general public. Many programs use them. The colorful brochure and handbook developed for the Texas A&M University Career Education Program for gifted and talented high school seniors, directed by William Nash, gives rich details about this year-long structured program. And Margaret Cellerino, a teacher of the gifted at the Harwinton School in Connecticut, has written a succinct brochure outlining the roles of mentor, student, and resource room teacher that can be very effective in a more fluid elementary style of program.

A comprehensive, one-page, photocopied, inexpensively reproduced brochure will work for you. Including one paragraph on each of the following items will give readers a concise overview of the program.

1. Program history

2. Program philosophy

3. Program components

4. Student selection process

5. Mentor role

6. Student role

7. Parent role

8. Coordinator role

It's even possible to include a community resource sign-up section within the brochure designed to allow the general public to indicate a willingness to serve the program in various capacities.

If you've concluded that developing a mentor program takes about as much energy and drive as working on a Herculean Ph.D., perhaps you're right. It won't happen overnight. And it won't happen within some administrator's predetermined, freeze-dried time frame.

Although the program development is not simple, at least the moral is. Change agents have to internalize Emerson's wisdom: Adopt the pace of nature. Her secret is patience.

The Final Word

In this book, we've attempted to share with you some important practical ideas about mentors and mentor programs, and to show you that research and experience both confirm the many positive outcomes of such experiences—for the mentors, the mentees, the school, and the community. Opportunities for students to experience mentor relationships are essential for creating balanced school programs that promote excellence, a matter of great concern for educators, policy-makers, and the public at large in our society.

Improving school programs requires more than just adding more hours to the school day, more days to the school year, or more subject requirements for graduation. Students who are learning to think critically and creatively and to solve problems effectively need challenges that go beyond doing the predictable exercises, worksheets, and textbook assignments. Bloom (1985) has demonstrated that those who attain significant levels of accomplishment in many fields are intensely and actively involved in their field over long periods of time (often years, not just weeks or months). Torrance (1984) emphasized the importance and need for students to "fall in love" with something, finding topics that offer excitement, challenge and stimulation that leads them to invest great time and effort in their work. Lasting mentor relationships lead to powerful results, which extend far beyond routine homework assignments or test grades, and which may influence the course or direction of the student's life goals, educational choices, and career goals.

Our schools (and many families) have traditionally placed a very narrow emphasis on indicators of success and expertise such as SAT scores, grades, and class rank. This overlooks the mentor option which gives students an opportunity to become stronger, more confidence and self-sufficient, as well as creatively productive. We sometimes forget the obvious—there is life before and after the SATs!

The practical value of significant mentorship experiences is clearly perceived by both college and university admissions officers and potential employers. Both groups report that the mentee has unusually attractive credentials.

But consider the issue from another angle. Torrance's (1984) research also showed that problems can result when people do not have mentoring opportunities. These included:

- Lack of career goal or focus

- Lack of enthusiasm or love for anything

- Missed opportunities

- Fear of pressures to conform

- Frustrated creativity

- Non-creative jobs that drain creative energy

- Emotional problems, drug or alcohol abuse

We believe strongly, then, that students who have opportunities for significant mentor experiences are likely to be stronger, healthier, and more competent personally and intellectually than students who do not have those opportunities.

And we sincerely hope that this book has given you the courage and motivation to cultivate mentor relationships, for yourself as well as the students in your school. Indeed, there can be many winners. And why not?

References

Bellflower, D.K., (1982). Developing a mentor relationship. *Roeper Review, 5*, 45-46.

Bloom, B., (Ed.) (1985). *Developing talent in young people.* New York: Ballantine.

Booth, L., (1980). Motivating gifted students through a shared-governance apprentice/mentor program. *Roeper Review, 3*, 11-13.

Boston, B. (1976). *The Sorcerer's Apprentice.* Reston, VA: Council for Exceptional Children.

Burger, C.R. & Schnur, J.O. (1981). The mentor approach - something for everyone, especially the gifted. *Roeper Review, 4,* 29-31.

Cellerino, M. (1983). A mentor-volunteer program for the gifted and talented. *Roeper Review, 6*, 45-46.

Cookingham, F.G. (1982). Community resources: a bit of philosophy. *Roeper Review, 5,* 2-4.

Crowe, M. & Walker J. (1977). *The current status of assessing experiential educational programs.* Columbus, OH: Ohio State University, National Center for Research in Vocational Education.

Digenakis, P. & Miller, J. (1979). What's my line? *Gifted Child Today Magazine, May / June,* 14-19.

Dettmer, P. (1980). The extended classroom: a gold mine for gifted students. *Journal for the Education of the Gifted, 3*, 133-142.

Eichberg, J. & Redmond, L. (1984). *Choosing and charting.* Honeoye, NY: Center for Creative Learning.

Empire State College (1978). Empire State College research series. Saratoga Springs, NY: Empire State College.

Feldhusen, J.F. & Treffinger, D.J. (1985). *Creative thinking and problem solving in gifted education.* (Third ed.) Dubuque, IA: Kendall-Hunt.

Goertzel, M.G., Goertzel, F., & Goertzel, T.F. (1978). *300 eminent personalities.* San Francisco, CA: Jossey-Bass.

Gray, W.A. (1982). Mentor-assisted enrichment projects for the gifted and talented. *Educational Leadership, 40,* 16-21.

Gross, R. (1982). *The independent scholar's handbook.* Reading, MA: Addison-Wesley, 1982.

Harris, R. (1984). Mentorship for the Gifted. *Gifted Child Today Magazine, May / June,* 8-9.

Hawk, M. & Tollefson, N. (1981). A para-educator model for gifted education. *Roeper Review, 4,* 35-37.

Hirsch, S. (1976). Executive High School internships. *Teaching Exceptional Children, Fall,* 22-23.

Isaksen, S.G. & Treffinger, D.J. (1985). *Creative problem solving: the basic course.* Buffalo, NY: Bearly Limited.

Jenkins, R. & Stewart, E. (1977). The community talent miner. In: J.S. Renzulli. *The enrichment triad model.* Mansfield Center, CT: Creative Learning Press. 84-86.

Korda, M. (1984). *Personnel Self, Sept.,* 48-50.

Lambert, S. & Lambert J. (1982). Mentoring: a powerful learning device. *Gifted Child Today Magazine, Nov. / Dec.,* 12-13.

Mattson, G. (1979). The mentorship for the gifted and talented: some practical considerations. *Gifted Child Today Magazine, May / June, Sept. / Oct.*

National Commission on Resources for Youth, Inc. (1978). Mentorship Newsletter. (February.)

Noller, R.B. (1982). *Mentoring: a voiced scarf.* Buffalo, NY: Bearly, Ltd.

Noller, R.B. & Frey, B.R. (1983). *Mentoring, an annotated bibliography.* Buffalo, NY: Bearly, Ltd.

Prichard, B. (1984). Wouldn't you like a mentor program, too? *Challenge, March/April,* 35-37.

Purdy, P. (1981). The great mentor hung: suggestions for the search. *Gifted Child Today Magazine, Jan./Feb.,* 19-20.

Redmond, L.T. (1984). *Pocketful of projects.* Honeoye, NY: Center for Creative Learning.

Renzulli, J.S. (1982). What makes a problem real? *Gifted Child Quarterly, 26,* 147-156.

Renzulli, J.S., Reis, S.M. & Smith, L.H. (1981). *The revolving door identification model.* Mansfield Center, CT: Creative Learning Press.

Runions, T. (1980). The Mentor Academy program: educating gifted/talented for the 80's. *Gifted Child Quarterly, 24,* 152-157.

Sarason, S. & Lorentz, E. (1979). *The challenge of the resource exchange network.* San Francisco, CA: Jossey-Bass.

Scobee, J. & Nash, W. (1983). A survey of highly successful space scientists concerning education for gifted and talented students. *Gifted Child Quarterly, 27,* 147-151.

Sweet, H.D. (1980). A mentor program: possibilities unlimited. *Gifted Child Today Magazine, Nov./Dec.,* 40-43.

Torrance, E.P. (1984). *Mentor relationships: how they aid creative achievement, endure, change, and die.* Buffalo, NY: Bearly, Limited.

Treffinger, D.J., Isaksen, S.G. & Firestien, R.L. (Eds.) (1982). *Handbook of Creative Learning: Volume 1.* Honeoye, NY: Center for Creative Learning.

The Mentor Kit
Forms Pack

Prufrock Press Post Office Box 8813
Waco, Texas 76714-8813
1-800-998-2208

Forms Pack Contents

The Community Connector

DNA
ACID RAIN
DANCE
MARKETING
ANIMAL MEDICINE
GEOGRAPHY
BANKING
PEACE CORPS
HORSEMANSHIP
ARCHITECTURE
ELECTRONICS
MATHEMATICS
COMMUNICATION
CULINARY ARTS
FISHING
ANTIQUING
WEATHER
COMPUTERS
ORNITHOLOGY
GENEALOGY
INVENTING
ARTS & CRAFTS
HISTORY
LAW
MARTIAL ARTS
WOODWORKING
POLITICS
ASTRONOMY
GARDENING
MUSIC
TAXIDERMY
COLLECTING
JOURNALISM
ARCHERY
CONSTRUCTION
PHOTOGRAPHY
BOATING
LANGUAGES
FARMING
MICROBIOLOGY
GOVERNMENT
SOCIAL WORK
LITERATURE
MEDIA
CONSERVATION
MEDICINE
THEATER
SPORTS
ENERGY
NUTRITION
ECONOMICS
COOKING
INDIAN LORE
TRAVEL
ENTOMOLOGY
BOTANY
GEOLOGY
ECOLOGY
ROBOTICS
ETCETERA

Those having torches will pass them on to others.
                    —*Plato,* Republic

Name(s): _____

Occupation: _____

Address: _____

Home Phone: _____ Business Phone: _____

Areas of Interest: Indicate, where possible, if lecture, demonstration, display, discussion, slides/movies, simulation, or "hands-on" activity are possible as part of your mentoring arrangement.

Amount of time you would be willing to devote: _____
     (single session)   (several sessions) (preferred length)
Number of students you prefer: 1   2-4   5-10   10+
Grade or age preferred: _____

When would you be available to work with students?
After school ___ Evenings ___ During day___ Saturdays___
Best day(s) of week: _____
Best time to call: Home: _____   Work: _____

Other information:
If you are a local resident, what is the name of the school nearest you?

Elementary School: _____
Middle School: _____
High School: _____

If you are currently a high school student, what high school do you attend, and in what year will you graduate?

The Mentor Contract

Name _____

Grade _____

Home Phone _____

Teacher _____

School Phone _____

Coordinator _____

Office Phone _____

Mentor _____

Business Phone _____

The Mentor Contract

Focus of research and responsibilities:

Skills:

Resources (including scholarly and professional) to be utilized:

Appropriate product and audience:

Plan of Action

Approximate beginning date _____ **Ending date** _____

Meeting dates with coordinators:
Dates & Times   **Comments**

_____   _____

_____   _____

_____   _____

_____   _____

_____   _____

_____   _____

_____   _____

_____   _____

Evaluation on a scale of 1-10 (1=Poor, 10=Excellent)

Criteria for evaluation	Student evaluation	Teacher evaluation
worked well independently	_____	_____
used a wide variety of resources	_____	_____
located scholarly resources	_____	_____
managed time and resources well	_____	_____
arranged for completion and sharing of product	_____	_____
provided bibliographic documentation	_____	_____
other _____	_____	_____
_____	_____	_____

Mentor Evaluation

In what technical and personal areas has your mentee demonstrated strength?

Mentee Comments

Coordinator Evaluation

How well did the student use a creative and organized approach in responding to the challenge?

Signatures

Student _____

Mentor _____

Coordinator _____

Parent _____

Project Checklist

Name of Project Director _____

Date Started _____

1. **Introduction.** You have been appointed project director for a project of your own. As you work on the project, you're becoming a specialist. You will have special knowledge and experience about your topic. In fact, when you're finished with the project, you will have done more interesting things, and you'll know more about it, than anyone else in your class—and quite possibly more than anyone else in the whole school!

   This project checklist is a guide to help you plan your project and carry it out successfully.

2. **What's your project?**

   Fill in the title of your project:

   Give a brief description of what your project will be about:

   What are some of the specific questions your project will investigate?

3. Project Consultants

Remember, you do not have to do this entire project all by yourself! There may be other people who will be able to assist you with the various parts of your project. We call these people consultants.

Here's a list of some people who might help you. In front of each name, there are two boxes. One is for you to check now, to make a note of some people you think might help you. Write their names in the spaces provided, if you wish. The second box is for you to check later, so you will be able to have a record of who really did give you help during the project.

There are also some blank lines for you to fill in the names of other people who may help you during the project.

You may come back to this step later—as often as necessary— to add names or bring it up to date.

❏ ❏ Teacher: _____   ❏ ❏ Teacher: _____
❏ ❏ Parent: _____   ❏ ❏ Parent: _____
❏ ❏ Friend: _____   ❏ ❏ Friend: _____
❏ ❏ Librarian: _____   ❏ ❏ Librarian: _____
❏ ❏ Business: _____   ❏ ❏ Business: _____
❏ ❏ _____   ❏ ❏ _____
❏ ❏ _____   ❏ ❏ _____

4. Meeting Dates

Use these spaces to keep a record of the meetings you have with the consultants who are assisting you. It would be a good idea to write down the date, the name of the person or people with whom you met, and a brief summary of what decisions you made in your meeting. (Add extra pages if you need them.)

Date	Met With	Decisions We Made

5. **Locating and Using Information.** Here are some ideas about how to locate and use some information for your project. In each list, there are two boxes. Your consultants may suggest that you use some of these ideas, by making checks in the first box. You can keep track of the ones you're using by placing checks in the second set of boxes. (Of course, you may check and use some things that your consultants didn't check—that's up to you.)

5a. Things to read/hear/view
❏ ❏ encyclopedias
❏ ❏ dictionaries
❏ ❏ textbooks
❏ ❏ biographies
❏ ❏ magazines
❏ ❏ almanacs
❏ ❏ bibliographies
❏ ❏ library card catalogs
❏ ❏ other books

❏ ❏ picture files
❏ ❏ charts
❏ ❏ graphs
❏ ❏ study packets
❏ ❏ records
❏ ❏ radio/TV programs
❏ ❏ newspapers
❏ ❏ maps
❏ ❏ _____

5b. Places to go
❏ ❏ libraries
❏ ❏ historical places
❏ ❏ business places
❏ ❏ concerts
❏ ❏ antique shops
❏ ❏ high schools
❏ ❏ art galleries
❏ ❏ public buildings
❏ ❏ shopping centers
❏ ❏ _____

❏ ❏ town halls
❏ ❏ museums
❏ ❏ outdoors
❏ ❏ theaters
❏ ❏ research laboratories
❏ ❏ colleges or universities
❏ ❏ zoos
❏ ❏ office buildings
❏ ❏ parks
❏ ❏ _____

5c. People to see/call/write
❏ ❏ teachers
❏ ❏ state officials
❏ ❏ businesses
❏ ❏ musicians
❏ ❏ professors
❏ ❏ librarians
❏ ❏ lawyers
❏ ❏ _____

❏ ❏ town officials
❏ ❏ national officials
❏ ❏ travel agents
❏ ❏ artists
❏ ❏ scientists
❏ ❏ reporters
❏ ❏ accountants
❏ ❏ _____

6. **Possible Products.** Here are some ideas for various products that might be the result of your project. These are different ways you might consider for sharing your project with other people. In the first box, you (with your consultants) can check some of the possibilities. Then, later, you can check the ones you've actually selected in the second set of boxes. (Some projects may have one product; others might lead to several products.)

❑ ❑ picture essay
❑ ❑ model to display
❑ ❑ mural/painting
❑ ❑ tape recording
❑ ❑ film
❑ ❑ slide/tape set
❑ ❑ posters
❑ ❑ newspaper story
❑ ❑ book or story
❑ ❑ sculpture
❑ ❑ school display
❑ ❑ campaign in our town/state/county
❑ ❑ _____
❑ ❑ _____

❑ ❑ magazine article
❑ ❑ diorama
❑ ❑ record
❑ ❑ videotape program
❑ ❑ filmstrip
❑ ❑ oral report
❑ ❑ bulletin board
❑ ❑ play
❑ ❑ written research report
❑ ❑ song/music
❑ ❑ presentation at a
    meeting of _____
❑ ❑ _____
❑ ❑ _____

7. **Planning Your Product(s).** In this space, write down some specific plans about your product and how you might be able to share it with others.

8. Collecting and Organizing Your Data.

After you have read what you need to read, visited the places of importance for your project, talked with the people whom you selected, and selected the kind of product(s) you will use for sharing your work, you need to be sure your material is well-organized.

Here are some resources you might use to help you organize your information and material: check those you're using.

_____ topic outline

_____ a list of main ideas

_____ questions and answers about your subject

_____ tape recorded notes and interviews

_____ file cards to record important ideas

_____ a list of the important steps in preparing your product

_____ picture or slide file in sequence

_____ rough draft of your product

9. Getting Ready for Sharing Your Product.

There are several questions you should be able to answer "yes" before your product is finished. Look over this list as a review before you complete your work. (Not every question will apply for every kind of product.) Check off the questions when you can answer "yes."

___Have I used many resources?
___Am I sure my information is accurate?
___Is the information concise and to the point?
___Have I eliminated unnecessary material?
___Do I feel comfortable with the subject?
___Have I organized my material in a logical sequence?
___Have I considered some especially interesting information to get the audience's attention?
___Am I using interesting charts, graphs, or illustrations?
___Can I "try out" my product with someone before it's finished?
___If I'm presenting, have I rehearsed my talk?
___Do I state my conclusions clearly and specifically?
___Have I arranged for all the materials I'll need?
___Do I know my deadlines?
___Is my project acceptable in size or length for the audience?
___Have I kept an extra copy for my own records?

10. Sharing Your Project. Use this space to keep a record of when, how, and where you have shared the results of your project.

When?   **How?**   **Where?**

_____

_____

_____

11. Evaluating Your Products.

After you have shared your project with others, you should ask, "How do I feel about the product?" Try to make a list of these things.

____ What things did you like best about this project and your products? (Try to find several things.)

____ What things did you like least about your project and products? (List several.)

____ Make a list of several things you will change or do in a different way the next time you share this project (or a future project) with an audience.

____ Make a list of helpful suggestions you have received from your consultants, or from the audiences for your products which will help you improve the products.

12. Where Do We Go From Here?

The most interesting thing about some projects is that answering one group of questions leads to a whole new set of questions and ideas. To conclude your checklist for this project, make a list of some new questions for future projects on this subject. Check some you especially hope to work on.

Date of completion of this project: _____

Evaluation of Mentor Placement

Name _____ Date _____

Mentor _____

Evaluation for period beginning _____ and ending _____

Evaluate your mentor placement by marking the scale in the most appropriate place for each item. For an item you believe needs improvement, please explain on the back of this form.

5=Excellent placement, most helpful
4=Very satisfactory
3=Adequate
2=Needs some improvement
1=Unsatisfactory; needs major improvement or change

My mentor is available; he or she is willing to help me when I need it	1 2 3 4 5
My mentor is patient and understanding	1 2 3 4 5
My mentor has a good sense of humor	1 2 3 4 5
My mentor is enthusiastic about his or her work	1 2 3 4 5
My mentor is enthusiastic about our meetings and work together	1 2 3 4 5
My mentor is able to teach me many new things	1 2 3 4 5
My mentor keeps appointments with me	1 2 3 4 5
My mentor keeps other commitments that are made to me	1 2 3 4 5
My mentor is willing to let me be independent and make decisions	1 2 3 4 5
My mentor tolerates my mistakes and helps me to learn from them	1 2 3 4 5
My mentor gives me clear directions	1 2 3 4 5
My mentor relates well to young people	1 2 3 4 5
My mentor has guided me and created new opportunities and experiences for me	1 2 3 4 5
I have learned about many things that are new to me through my mentor	1 2 3 4 5
My mentor helps me to develop ideas and plans for future projects	1 2 3 4 5
My mentor helps me to clarify or to create future career opportunities	1 2 3 4 5
Other:	1 2 3 4 5